Discovering
Your Purpose

Discovering Your Purpose

Ivy Haley

SkillPath Publications

Mission, Kansas

Project Editor: Kelly Scanlon

Editor: Jane Doyle Guthrie

Page Layout and Design: Rod Hankins and David Sherer

Sculpture and Cover Design: Rod Hankins

Library of Congress Catalog Card Number: 95-74668

ISBN: 1-878542-92-3

10 9 8 7 6 5 4   03   04   05   06

Printed in the United States of America

To

Skip Haley

Victoria Ausonio

Knight Berman, Jr.

whose encouragement and timely help

made this book possible.

Many thanks also to

Dr. Dee Jones Adams

and

Patrick Wood

"I'm gonna fly from my cocoon and put my footsteps on the moon."

—*Dr. Denis Waitley*
The Psychology of Winning

"Definiteness of Purpose: The knowledge of what you want, and a burning desire to possess it."

—*Napolean Hill*
Think and Grow Rich

Contents

Introduction 1

1 Your Inventory of Pleasurable Activities 5

2 Your Inventory of Abilities 17

3 Your Inventory of Values and Principles 25

4 Discovering Your Deep Desires 37

5 Your Career Path 49

6 Sketching a Blueprint of Your Life Plan 61

7 Your Life Plan and Statement of Purpose 79

8 The Case for Goals 89

9 Visualization and Thought-Talk 113

10 Reflecting on the Process 119

Bibliography and Suggested Reading 123

Introduction

Are you getting what you want out of life? Do you know what you really want? Or do you feel like one professional who said: "I've been watching my life go by through windows: windows in my office, windows in my automobile, and Windows in my computer."

It's so easy to get caught on an activity rollercoaster, entrapped in the "busy"-ness of life and achieving empty victories. Waking up to find that success has come at the expense of something more valuable is a startling realization. Many people struggle to achieve greater income, status, recognition, or competence, only to find as they moved along that they were blinded to what mattered most. The goal they achieved proved barren in the end.

Your life can be likened to a jigsaw puzzle with many parts and pieces. No one would attempt to put a jigsaw puzzle together without first looking at the big picture. Yet, we attempt to live our lives without a plan—without a life map and a clearly stated purpose—without the big picture. We may strike down one path only to retreat to another. Many people spend more time planning a vacation than they do planning their lives.

What's needed is a map of the roads you want to travel in life, a design for the journey you want to take, and a plan for how to get there. Ask yourself whether or not you have a clear sense of direction and purpose that inspires and energizes you. Is there something that wakes you up fresh and ready for the day? Or are you indefinite about what is important to you and uncertain about what you really want from life?

How different your life becomes when you establish your purpose and use it as a frame of reference for planning, setting goals, and examining tasks and behaviors. How altered your direction when you really know what is deeply valuable, and keep that picture firmly in mind—when you become and do what matters most. Every step you take toward determining your purpose gets you to the right place faster. It's not just a mind exercise, although it does require a lot of thought. And it involves the total person to discover total purpose.

This book isn't about selecting the most extravagant thing you can imagine and pursuing it as your purpose. Statistically it's been shown that conventional lives are the happiest. Everyday mundane activities have a direct relationship to happiness if they're designed as pleasurable daily rituals. Ordinary disciplines like exercise, hard work, eating properly, not smoking, and working at a relationship all play their part. Balance is essential. Dedicating too much of yourself in one direction may leave too little for enjoyment in another. The lopsided struggle for outer trappings—wealth and power—can cause you to lose focus of what's really important. The focus here is investing yourself in those things that matter most to you, that bring internal as well as external success, things like personal fulfillment, pride, and passion. Like paying attention to your inner identity, and taking care to discover your wants and desires.

As you proceed through the exercises that follow, you'll investigate a number of possibilities for yourself from an armchair position. In an exploratory, imaginative excursion, you'll identify what you'd most love to do, to be, and to possess. The building blocks you discover won't require immediate action other than reflective sifting, considering, and decision making. You can experiment through your imagination and visualize your growth. You can try your ideas on for size and then choose those that best propel you toward your goals.

It's important that you move at your own pace through the book. As you take on each group of stimulating exercises, you'll find that you're taking larger steps more easily, and you'll trust yourself more fully to discern what you really do want. You probably will also notice less of an urge to consult others whose opinions you may have depended upon in the past, because you'll obtain critical information that will help you move with certainty in taking charge of your life.

The purpose you finally designate for yourself doesn't necessarily have to be an all-consuming mission that aims for the stars, but it does need to be dynamic and sufficiently powerful to provide a steady, progressive challenge. It's not the size of your purpose that matters, but rather how accurately it captures your deepest "raison d'être." What drives you? What gets your wheels turning and gets you going each day? What are your passions? Step by step, within the guided framework of this book, you'll uncover your purpose. And that in turn will very naturally offer you direction, focus, and perspective in your life. Purpose is a singular, compelling force. It shapes our destiny and gives us a stronger sense of completeness. You now stand at the threshold; new paths are beckoning ahead. It's time to begin.

Chapter 1

Your Inventory of Pleasurable Activities

"Whenever you are sincerely pleased,

you are nourished."

—Ralph Waldo Emerson

Imagine yourself getting old. That's right: white-haired or no-haired, walking more slowly, stooping a bit, with creaks and groans a way of life.

Looking for a transforming tonic? Something that could hold back the sands of time?

The tonic is a strong, dynamic purpose. This can often produce a revitalizing effect. Purpose doesn't make old people younger, but try telling that to them! Seniors have been seen to come fully alive while working on priorities they relish, projects that represent immense value to them and to which they commit heart and soul. They move resolutely through their work, firing their enthusiasm through creativity and absorption. There's a passion in such people, one that's rooted in the unadulterated satisfaction of doing what's most enjoyable. It's the pleasure and delight of the work, the zeal and the ardor, that makes the difference. And it doesn't take genius or astounding creativity to metamorphose in this way. Normal, everyday people may well encounter this experience when they're doing the things they love most, for doing what we love has a rejuvenating effect.

Having a firm handle on what you truly enjoy can also help you avoid making big mistakes. For example, you may realize that a certain promotion might not bring more job satisfaction; by scaling down the enjoyment factor, it might actually bring less. If you thrive on managing details and statistics, that knowledge might help you realize that you'd hate meeting the public all day, with little time on your computer. If you're gregarious, you might feel claustrophobic being alone and bound to a desk. Look at the different aspects of your life and see where the pleasures lie.

Think first of the simple activities that please you. These don't have to fall in with anyone else's idea of fun, nor do they have to be "in" things to do. All the small pleasures count here—taking a walk, playing with your pet, reading, gardening. Make a decision right now to enjoy and cultivate the most positive emotions and activities you can think of. Understand that you deserve to experience them daily. Realize that enjoyment can be used as a tool to reduce stress. The bottom line with stress is "energy out." Hobbies, playtime, laughter shared with friends—all these aid in building "energy in."

It's important to make time for what you enjoy most. If you love classical music but don't listen or play because urgent activities crowd your day, if it's your passion to visit art museums but you never take the time, if you love to laugh with your friends but feel too busy to get together with them, you may well be on your way to becoming a "pleasure anorexic"—someone who has difficulty taking time out for life's really enjoyable moments. Such people feel they have no right to pursue joy, so they don't allow themselves to. Or they're so stressed they don't have time for it. Both feel guilty for enjoying themselves simply for enjoyment's sake, and apathy and zestlessness are the predictable consequences.

Where do we get the idea that it is noble to suppress our dreams, to obliterate our desires? The spiritual concept of "denying yourself" has so often been misinterpreted or misrepresented. What a grievous mistake! While license and narcissism aren't wise, really knowing yourself, realizing your value, and enjoying your life are essential achievements. And there's also something to be said about *appropriate* self-denial—it's conducive to high self-esteem, and it's a part of being true to yourself. If you can say "no" to yourself about something you want, realizing it's inappropriate, you're exerting control over yourself. Whether you're investing or dieting or whatever else to attain a goal, self-denial provides a sense of congruence. And that sense of being in balance and harmony is pleasurable in itself. It can also be a reason to reward yourself for good behavior, with some incentive or pleasurable activity.

If you haven't grasped life with all its fullness, if you've forgotten the things you love to do, then do yourself a favor and reidentify them now. It's up to you to choose more joy, more fun, more confidence and peace of mind.

Inventory of Pleasurable Experiences

A. Spend a few relaxed moments remembering the most pleasant experiences of your past. Jot down a sentence that deals with these experiences, and as you do, think about the things that specifically caused you to experience joy on that occasion:

1. _____

_____

2. _____

_____

3. _____

_____

4. _____

_____

5. _____

_____

6. _____

_____

7. _____

_____

Any common elements: _____

_____

_____

B. As you continue considering the benefits of having pleasure in your life, list by category some day-to-day activities that you enjoy:

Family Activities

_____

_____

_____

_____

_____

_____

_____

_____

Relationship Activities

_____

_____

_____

_____

_____

_____

_____

_____

_____

_____

Work Situations and Challenges

_____

_____

_____

_____

_____

_____

_____

_____

_____

_____

_____

Outdoor/Indoor Activities

_____

_____

_____

_____

_____

_____

_____

_____

_____

_____

_____

_____

Recreational Activities

_____

_____

_____

_____

_____

_____

_____

_____

_____

_____

Individual Activities

_____

_____

_____

_____

_____

_____

_____

_____

_____

_____

Other

_____

_____

_____

_____

_____

_____

_____

_____

_____

_____

_____

C. You can begin by taking steps, no matter how small or insignificant, in the right direction. The objective here is to identify the things you most enjoy, from life's little pleasures to those that fire your life. Here are some more questions to ask yourself:

1. What is really important to you?_____

_____

_____

_____

_____

_____

_____

2. What were you doing the last time you felt really satisfied? _____

_____

_____

_____

_____

_____

_____

_____

3. The people you know who enjoy themselves most: _____

_____

_____

_____

_____

_____

_____

_____

4. They seem to enjoy themselves because: _____

_____

_____

_____

_____

_____

_____

5. What are you like when you are at your best? _____

_____

_____

_____

_____

_____

_____

6. What is it about you that makes you glad to be who you are? _____

_____

_____

_____

_____

_____

_____

7. What actions, activities, and possessions do you find particularly enjoyable? _____

_____

_____

_____

_____

_____

_____

8. If you dreamed a perfect day, what would it be like?

_____

_____

_____

_____

_____

_____

_____

_____

_____

_____

_____

_____

9. As you think about the things you enjoy, what accomplishments come to mind? _____

_____

_____

_____

_____

_____

_____

_____

_____

_____

_____

_____

Now that you have an inventory of pleasurable activities and accomplishments, hold on to them; you'll be coming back to them later in the book. In the meantime, make sure you incorporate these activities into your life. Choose them over activities that bring only thrills and excitement, that can become addictive or unsatisfying over the long run. Keep in mind that many of the most pleasurable activities include serving others and looking to the greater good. Joy itself is associated with positively affecting the lives of others.

Chapter 2

Your Inventory of Abilities

"There is something that is much more scarce, something finer far, something rarer than ability. It is the ability to recognize ability."

—*Elbert Hubbard*

Each of us is endowed with specific talents and abilities that are programmed into our very being. These attributes aren't acquired: they're natural to us, "written in" before we're born. You can take a step toward determining your purpose by discovering your unique talents and skills, especially those that cause you joy when you use them.

Your *ability,* your "power to do something," represents the sum of your aptitudes and skills. *Aptitudes* are natural inclinations and special talents, those things you do by "second nature" that are sometimes referred to as "gifts." Examples of aptitudes might include such things as the ability to remember numbers, faces, or names easily; athletic ability or dexterity of some sort; an ear for music; or a knack for creating designs and visualizing three-dimensionally.

You'll be happier overall if you design activities for yourself that flow naturally from your aptitudes and from the skills you've clustered around those aptitudes. You may have formed an idea of some of your abilities since completing the last chapter's lists of pleasurable activities and accomplishments—they're highly related to your talents and skills. Spend some time now to carefully reflect on your abilities and aptitudes. The exercise that follows will guide your thinking.

Inventory of Aptitudes and Abilities

A. Aptitudes are inherent; they're those things you naturally do easily and well. In the following spaces, name at least five aptitudes or talents you see in yourself:

_____

_____

_____

_____

_____

_____

_____

B. Following are some questions that will help you further investigate your basic talents and abilities:

1. What courses did you like most in school?_____

_____

_____

_____

_____

_____

_____

_____

2. What topics do you talk the most about? _____

_____

_____

_____

_____

_____

_____

3. What do you like to do on weekends? _____

_____

_____

_____

_____

_____

_____

4. What clubs or organizations have you been interested in joining? _____

_____

_____

_____

_____

_____

_____

The questions you've just answered will shine a light on your aptitudes. Bottom-line: aptitudes come into play when you are performing a mental or physical task with enjoyment. If you are not enjoying the task at hand, you may lack the skills to do the job well or perhaps the aptitude for it. Aptitude deficits present additional information about yourself. Someone who ranks high in manual dexterity, for example, may enjoy piano playing and computer games. However if that person ranked low in the ability to rapidly move the eyes, he or she would be easily frustrated with either activity because hand-eye coordination is necessary. Someone who is low in forethought—the aptitude that deals with long-range planning and looking to the future—will not be as inclined to play chess or plan for retirement.

A *skill*, on the other hand, has been defined as an art, a trade, or a technique that allows you to accomplish a goal. In it's simplest definition, a skill is something you've *learned* to do—a developed ability, like reading. Riding a motorcycle, changing a flat tire, and scrambling eggs are all skills. So are ironing a shirt, developing a vaccine, tuning an engine, or repairing an artery—in the city's infrastructure or in the human body. These are all skills.

As noted, you can reveal your aptitudes by paying attention to what you are naturally good at and enjoy doing. And you can develop and maximize your talents by building skills in clusters around them. For instance, suppose you have a singing voice that performs the grandest operatic scales—in the shower. You may be naturally inclined to sing as you bathe, and it may be quite good, but if you haven't developed the skills it takes to be a performer, your only audience might be your rubber ducky. Likewise, if you have a lawnmower and you know how to use it, you could certainly mow a yard without much trouble. However, if you aren't naturally inclined toward landscape maintenance, your work may wear the mark of apathy, and you won't derive much satisfaction from it either. Aptitudes are like diamonds in the rough; it's only when they're polished through skill development that you have the glowing gem.

Inventory of Skills and Accomplishments

A. The following list of skills is not all-inclusive, but it will give you ample material to draw from. Most people have scores of skills. Use the spaces below the lists to record some of your skills:

Accounting	Ad-libbing	Analyzing
Asserting yourself	Budgeting	Caring for children
Carrying out details	Coaching	Communicating
Computing	Cooking	Coordinating
Crafting	Creating	Decorating
Delegating	Drawing	Initiating action
Instructing	Interviewing	Listening
Managing time	Motivating others	Nursing
Operating machinery	Organizing	Persuading
Planning	Problem solving	Promoting
Reading	Relaxing	Repairing things
Selling	Speaking in public	Supervising
Training	Visualizing	Writing

_____   _____   _____

_____   _____   _____

_____   _____   _____

_____   _____   _____

_____   _____   _____

B. Now list some of your accomplishments. As you remember them, you may notice a pattern—your achievements were probably in areas where your aptitudes were enhanced by skills.

If you can't think of where your strongest aptitudes and skills meet in a happy union, think back to your childhood and your most pleasurable activities during that purer, unadulterated time. No matter what the game, did you enjoy the company of playmates just for the camaraderie? Or did you find more bliss alone, say building a model airplane or decorating a dollhouse? It's possible the memories may be a bit cloudy, so allow yourself enough time for adequate contemplation.

You may find yourself remembering past accomplishments that you have long forgotten. Continue thinking about these accomplishments and follow them from your childhood to the present. Refer to your previous list—you'll generally find aptitudes and their skill clusters at the root of your successes. Make notes below as you're thinking.

1. Accomplishment _____

_____

_____

Aptitude and Skills _____

_____

_____

2. Accomplishment _____

_____

_____

Aptitude and Skills _____

_____

_____

3. Accomplishment _____

_____

_____

Aptitude and Skills _____

_____

_____

4. Accomplishment _____

_____

_____

Aptitude and Skills _____

_____

_____

5. Accomplishment _____

_____

_____

Aptitude and Skills _____

_____

_____

6. Accomplishment _____

_____

_____

Aptitude and Skills _____

_____

_____

Chapter 3

Your Inventory of Values and Principles

"He is rich or poor according to what he is, not according to what he has."

—*Henry Ward Beecher*

Values guide your life. A value is your concept of something desirable in and of itself—it's your inner imperative. Values are standards that you attach importance to; they're obvious to others through your personality traits, and they differ from person to person. They influence your choice of friends, activities, and work. Having a ready grasp of your values allows you to focus on direction and purpose; otherwise, you'll likely experience conflict, manage your time poorly, and make decisions in a somewhat random fashion.

We experience inner conflict when our behaviors oppose our values. If our decisions aren't aligned with our values, a sense of discomfort and uneasiness results. Psychologists call this phenomenon "cognitive dissonance"—acting in a way that doesn't feel right. The process makes you feel squirmy inside; it goes against the grain. If you value health and a muscular physique, then failing to exercise or overloading on sweets will likely make you feel uneasy. If you value maintaining a close relationship with your spouse or child but then spend most off-work hours watching TV, you will feel dissatisfied. If you value integrity but are urged to cheat by someone you feel you can't say "no" to, you will experience unease and anxiety.

You can generally tell whether your decisions are consistent with your values by your level of contentment. You have more peace of mind when your behaviors align with your value structure. And being in harmony with your deepest values is essential to establish a sense of purpose and direction.

It's important to re-examine your values periodically. People who don't can find themselves propelled by values that no longer serve them. For example, if you value cleaning your plate because as a child you heard about starving children, you may realize that value puts you in conflict with your plan for dieting. If you find yourself looking at a particular behavior and asking, "Why am I doing this?" you need to investigate what underlies it. In other words, it's imperative to question your values and recast those that aren't serving you well.

Our personal values influence the decisions we make both *intuitively* and *intellectually*. A person might, for example, purchase a flashy sportscar because he or she values attention or adventure or feeling young again. The car represents a means to that end—although the person may be unable to afford it. Knowing the value behind the manifestation is helpful, because there are other, less expensive ways to satisfy the need for attention, adventure, and feeling youthful without spending beyond your budget.

It's wise to look for the underlying value, to prod beyond the surface reason and uncover the more substantive motive. Clarity at this point facilitates decision making and enables you to grasp what is truly important before making a significant mistake.

This clarification process is critical to effective time management, for if you know your values, you can choose to spend time on your most important agendas. Time management principles of the past were based on prioritizing "urgent" activities, but a more effective method bases these principles on *values*. Simply stated, you determine what you value most and that's where you spend your time.

Inventory of Values and Principles

A. Purposeful living doesn't accommodate being the master of the wrong details. Answer the following questions to bring your values into clearer focus.

1. What four things are most important to you? _____

_____

_____

_____

_____

_____

2. What are some things you've really wanted but never dared to go for?

_____

_____

_____

_____

_____

3. What, specifically, are you willing to give your life to?_____

_____

_____

_____

_____

_____

4. In what areas of your life do you spend the most time? What activity do you spend the most time doing?

_____

_____

_____

_____

_____

5. Do you find enjoyment in the areas where you spend the most time? If not, what's causing you to spend so much time in those areas? _____

_____

_____

_____

_____

6. In what areas do you desire to spend more time than you're spending?

_____

_____

_____

_____

_____

7. What are the most valuable aspects of your job or career? _____

_____

_____

_____

_____

8. If you were to defend or support something you believe in, what would it be? _____

_____

_____

_____

_____

9. What character qualities do you find admirable in others? _____

_____

_____

_____

_____

_____

10. What are the things you do, or could do, that would be of most value to others? _____

_____

_____

_____

_____

_____

B. At the bottom of the page, you'll see a list of twenty-five values laid out in block fashion. Take a moment to place a large "X" in the block that contains a value you can live your life without. Although at first you may feel that all these values are significant, some will stand out as obviously more important than others. So, look again and cross through several more.

Now get ruthless. Cross through all the remaining values, except for ten.

Congratulations. Now mark down to seven.

Dig in—you're almost there. Cross through more values until just five remain on the page.

These are your five highest values. How these values are aligned greatly impact your decisions and your conduct.

Values Grid

Accomplishment	Adventure	Affection	Approval	Challenge
Competition	Family	Freedom	Health	Financial Security
Independence	Integrity	Loyalty	Order	Relationships
Recognition	Prestige	Power	Security	Self-Acceptance
Spiritual	Wealth	Wisdom	Pleasure	Self-Development

Fill in the blanks as you participate in this written scenario to determine the ascending order of your five highest values:

You've just been diagnosed with an incurable disease and told you have six months to live. Unwilling to accept this news, you spend the next several weeks searching for a cure.

Hearing of a possible new miracle drug, you fly across the country to obtain it. When you arrive, you're told that just one dose of the drug will provide the relief you seek—in exchange for one of your values. Filled with anticipation of the drug's "curing" powers, you give up_____ (select one of the five).

You take the drug and wait for your symptoms to disappear, your good health to return. It doesn't happen. A month has passed. You have only four months to live. Reading a magazine one day, you see an ad for yet another possible cure. Again, you pursue the lead, only to find you must give up another value. You give up

_____ .

Discovering weeks later that the "cure" does not heal you, you desperately seek out a naturalist known for his healing powers. He agrees to "counsel" you in exchange for one of your values. You give up _____ .

Filled with new hope, you follow the naturalist's regimen for one month. There's no improvement.

Thinking that a change in eating habits might reverse your fortunes, you seek out a new diet. You discover that there is a diet that has helped others in your condition. But to find out the details, you must give up another value_____ .

To your horror, your condition worsens. Just as you finally begin to accept your terminal condition, you hear of yet another "cure" for your illness. Desperately seeking information about the plan and entering the last weeks of your life, you give up your final value

_____.

The last value you hold onto is ranked Number 1. List the other four now in descending order, Number 5 being the one you gave up first in the story:

1. _____

2. _____

3. _____

4. _____

5. _____

C. Ask yourself two questions now:

- Is what I am doing now bringing me closer to or further away from my major values?

- What's important to me about each of these values?

Value #1 _____

_____

_____

Value #2 _____

_____

_____

Value #3 _____

_____

_____

Value #4 _____

_____

_____

Value #5 _____

_____

_____

People with direction are typically those with a defined set of values and beliefs. A value offers a rationale for *why you do what you do*. Knowing and living according to your values also contributes to peace of mind. Knowing your values helps facilitate your ability to make decisions and helps reduce stress by letting you focus precious time and energy on what means the most to you. This knowledge is essential to goal setting, and it allows you to feel better about making the tough choices. Our ability to have "fun" is also tied up with personal values and beliefs. When you know what you value, you can maximize your pleasure.

As you learn your own values, train yourself to be observant of others' values in order to deal with them more effectively. For example, if your boss values order, tranquillity, and stability, then asking for something or presenting problems in a noisy environment may precipitate a confrontation. Although someone else's values may not coincide with your own, keep in mind that those values are meaningful to that person. And knowing those values gives you a tool in dealing with that person.

Certain key principles have guided countless generations and remain relevant for us today; such values (honesty, integrity, respect, equality, excellence, kindness, faith, fair-play, accountability, quality, and unconditional love) serve as universal truths. The golden rule, which urges us to do unto others as we would have them do unto us, falls into this category. Some people mistakenly think that this perspective would put them at a disadvantage, but nothing could be further from the truth. Actions that arise from principle produce good personal feelings, and generate an appropriate regard for and love of self. Not a selfish demanding love, but one that comes from sticking to values and principles. When you're principle-centered, driven by and operating out of your values, you experience far greater life fulfillment.

Keep in mind that a clear purpose identifies where you want to go, according to what you value most. Discerning your own personal values and using behaviors that are in harmony with your value structure enables you to be proactive, to act on important issues rather than react to circumstances. People without values lack focus and tend to choose the "meandering around" method of living. Directionless lives aren't the happiest to look back upon, and it's well to determine to be both someone *with* values as well as someone *of* value.

Chapter 4

Discovering Your Deep Desires

"It is difficult to say what is impossible,
for the dream of yesterday is the hope of
today and the reality of tomorrow."

—Robert H. Goddard

It's clear by now that every life needs a direction, a purpose. Without it we drift, often uncomfortably. One reason many people lack direction in life is because they lack connection with their own dreams and deep desires. In *On Walden Pond,* philosopher Henry David Thoreau wrote, "If one advances confidently in the direction of his dreams, and endeavors to live the life which he has imagined, he will meet with a success unexpected in common hours."

People who know where they're going wake up in the morning to carry out their dreams and enjoy their lives. They have meaningful contact with others and live with a sense of fulfillment. They're stimulated to attempt new challenges as they're swept along by their own passionate curiosity and interest. Unfortunately, though, an overwhelming majority of those around us have only a vague idea of where they are going in life, or why they are alive. They get up in the morning to go to work and then come home to relax and go to bed, only to get up again tomorrow and begin all over again. This process is often accompanied by a vague sense of uneasiness or downright unhappiness. Often these people focus on the "shoulds" of life instead of following their own desires.

Plans in life that are established by the *"shoulds"* and *"oughts"* almost always run off course:

- "I should take this job because it means more money."

- "I should stay with this company because my parents/family/friends think it's a good idea."

- "I should be in the medical profession—my dad was a doctor."

- "I should pursue this direction because there are openings in the field."

Such belief statements will hinder your progress if they're not founded on deeply held desires and convictions. Among the questions you need to ask yourself are:

- Why am I doing what I'm doing (regarding work, relationships, etc.)?

- What prompted me to begin in the first place?

When you blindly follow "shoulds" and "oughts" because you haven't determined your own purpose, you'll sense that you're compromising yourself. The days may range from slightly dull to downright boring as you zigzag along, buffeted by circumstances. How many people do you know who are in jobs or careers because they thought that's what they "should" be doing? Often the "shoulds" are layered across our imagination, blocking our creative ability to determine our truest passion and unearth our deepest desires. What a price we pay for them!

Oliver Wendell Holmes once said: "The biggest tragedy in America is not the waste of natural resources, though this is tragic. The biggest tragedy is the waste of human resources." And how are these resources wasted? "The average person goes to his grave with his music still in him." Imagine that—leaving this world while the melody of your life goes unsung—settling for complacency, pursuing the Pied Piper of "oughts" and "shoulds."

Another hindrance to acting on our deep desires are internal myths about our talents, strengths, and abilities. For example, some of us believe that we have a poor sense of direction, or little sense of style, or lack the ability to converse well with others. We feel anxiety as we contemplate these weaknesses. Some of them may not be weaknesses at all, however—just firmly implanted (and often ill-founded) fallacies that stifle us.

A study involving incoming freshmen at UCLA asked the students to divide a page in half and then write all their strengths/positives on one side and all their weaknesses/negatives on the other. Which half do you think contained the larger number? The average ratio was six negatives for every positive. *Six to one!* That may not be surprising, considering our fairly common tendency to speak negatively to ourselves and to others about ourselves. After all, our parents taught us not to brag.

Actually, we can learn important lessons by taking an objective look at our supposed deficits. Close examination may reveal some erroneous notions that we, or others, have planted in our minds over a period of time, and we need to ask ourselves whether these weaknesses truly exist.

While we often set up well-entrenched blocks that keep us from tuning in to our deepest desires, there are creative ways around these obstacles. One takes place through *constructive dreaming,* which enables you to reach into hidden depths of memory's treasure chest. Using your imagination, think of the time when you were least inhibited, back when you were a child. Take a few moments to close your eyes and picture yourself as a two- or three-year-old, back in those days when you would see something you wanted and just go after it. You'd see a shiny object, and your mind and energy would merge into a single, focused thought: *gimme.* And you'd scramble toward it. Ignoring obstacles in your path, paying little attention to the "no" you may have heard in the background—your goal was set, and you became a dynamo of forward motion. Earlier, when parents held out their hands to you and coaxed you to come—even though the piece of furniture you were clutching seemed safe and secure, and you may also have been scared—you risked taking those wobbly, uncertain steps. You were propelled by your desire and undeterred in your purpose. And if you fell, you may have been indignant, but you did not give up. You never said, "I'm not good at this—I just don't have the talent" or "Gee, this is hard. I'll never make it, and I'm not even gonna try." No—you were determined, and you had your own very definite ideas.

As a matter of fact, as a child you probably had some ideas about what you'd do or be when you grew up! Maybe a fireman or an astronaut or...

"I'll be a movie star."

"I'll be a famous ballet dancer."

"I'll be President of the United States."

What You Might Have Been

Write down a sentence describing what you might have been. If it's difficult to remember your childhood dreams and fantasies, the toys and games you preferred can also provide clues. Just think: what might you have been? What were the things you dreamed of doing? Think big. Be as extravagant and far-fetched as you wish. Let your mind run free to those early dreams, to the time when your reveries were unpolluted by do's and don'ts.

_____

_____

_____

_____

_____

_____

_____

_____

_____

_____

_____

Now look over your answer. Remember, this isn't about *reality*, it's about *fantasy*. It's about dreaming, because it is through constructive, creative, lavish dreaming that we discover our deep desires.

In the midst of all this child's play, this fantasizing and imagining, let's not forget that "shoulds" and "oughts" are often deeply entrenched. Internal myths and ill-founded notions take time to alter. Effort is required to unearth these obstructions, to sort through them, and to deal with them in reality. But with your imagination, through constructive dreaming, you can leap past self-limiting messages and determine your deepest wishes. The process used to plumb the depths of those desires is called the "do-be-possess" method of pre-goal setting. It's a simple and delightful task that involves making three separate lists:

- If I could *do* anything in the world, what would I do?

- If I could *be* anything, what would I be?

- If I *could* possess anything, what would I have?

The important thing is to let your imagination soar. Don't hinder yourself in any way. If you thought, "If I could possess anything, I'd have a 5,000-square-foot home overlooking the Pacific Ocean in Maui, Hawaii, *but of course I can't afford that,*" then get rid of that condemning, limiting "I can't afford it" and just write down the home. Do the same with any limiting thoughts that show up, like "I'd do that, but I don't have the education," or "I'm too old," or "I'm not smart enough." Throw those out! Don't allow yourself to use those restricting phrases. But say you thought, "If I could be anything in the world, I'd be an opera star"—but you can't sing a note. Don't throw that out! Why? Because there's something there that attracts you, and that may be a valid message for you today. Maybe you are musically oriented, or you have a hidden on-stage personality—perhaps there's a big ham inside waiting to emerge. Don't judge the creative ideas that dance across your mind; welcome them and write them down. They're valuable "messages."

Over the next few pages you'll have a chance to explore the "do-be-possess" method for yourself as you complete the "Inventory of Deep Desires." Don't hold back! Sometimes it's difficult to give ourselves permission to freely express everything we'd like to be or do. For example, "I'd like to be a celebrity in the community" gets thrown out because it sounds conceited. Hold it. Don't limit yourself! You must commit to being honest with yourself as you do the exercise. And what about those things you'd like to possess? Realize that most of us desire to have harmonious work relationships, a comfortable home, the respect of family and peers, good health, security in our careers and personal lives, and so on. But don't forget "things." Don't hesitate to express everything you'd possibly want to own. And don't feel guilty listing them!

Don't expect to come up with everything at your first sitting. Jot some ideas down now. Then take a break. Go to a park, sit by a river, or maybe look out a window with a pleasing view. Go anywhere that will give you inspiration—and take this book with you.

Inventory of Deep Desires

Allow yourself the luxury of dreaming, of imagining, of seeing yourself ecstatic as you become whatever you want to be, do whatever you want to do, and have whatever you wish to possess.

Take time to do this exercise, completing the questions on the next few pages thoroughly. You will likely need to return to your previous lists on several occasions. Keep in mind that this exercise is freeing your imagination from the obstacles of limiting personal scenarios, myths about your abilities, and the burden of the "shoulds" and "oughts." It may well be the most important exercise you encounter in defining direction for your life.

1. If I could do anything, I would…

_____

_____

_____

_____

_____

_____

_____

_____

_____

_____

_____

_____

_____

_____

_____

_____

_____

_____

2. If I could be anything, I would be...

_____

_____

_____

_____

_____

_____

_____

_____

_____

_____

_____

_____

_____

_____

_____

_____

_____

_____

_____

3. If I could possess anything, I'd possess...

_____

_____

_____

_____

_____

_____

_____

_____

_____

_____

_____

_____

_____

_____

_____

_____

_____

_____

_____

You have completed a great deal of important work here. You'll be returning to it often as you set your goals and sketch out the blueprint for your life's plan.

Chapter 5

Your Career Path

*"Nothing is really work unless
you would rather be doing
something else."*

—James Matthew Barrie

Although occupation doesn't equal purpose, certainly a large portion of your time is spent at work, and analyzing your career goals naturally asserts itself as a part of determining your mission. As you plan your life, you'll want to carefully weave career threads into the fabric of your purpose. Work connected with purpose can be a sustaining and integral part of life, and it can become increasingly pleasurable just as naturally as seeds nudging up from the ground turn their faces to the sun. Work can become a "good times" experience when you're doing something you love, something that mirrors your values and your purpose.

Throughout our work experiences, all of us are likely to look instinctively for what we feel we were born to do. We sense there is a particular calling or vocation meant for us alone, one that will fulfill our deepest longing and reflect our inner selves. The majority of us strive for meaning in our lives and embark on a lifelong voyage to find it. We want our work to have significance, to be a gratifying experience that helps us grow into enlightened and caring people. But even fulfilling work will have its share of frustration and irritation, of ups and downs. And it demands our time.

Whether you're in a steppingstone position or have actualized the dream job itself, gauge the "fulfillment" aspect of it by asking some questions:

- In the overall scheme of things, what contribution am I making?

- What will be the value of the hours and years I'm spending when I look back on my life?

- In what ways is my work helping the people around me?

Work that is fulfilling looks to the greater good. There can be great satisfaction, for example, for a teacher who's prompting and motivating students to learn and to gain confidence, or for an indispensable assistant who shapes the office to accomplish the company's mission and stated purpose, or for an employee who believes in what the company is accomplishing and contributes to that greater good. But what if you feel you're simply knee-deep in the drudgery of keeping unruly students in line, or think of yourself as "just" a secretary who types and files or "just" an employee getting through each day in order to leave on time? Looking to the greater good of your job greatly influences how you feel about your work.

If someone asks you "Is this what you want to do for the rest of your life?" and your answer is "no," then you're automatically at a crossroads, faced with the decision either to play it safe or to find what you really want. If you're not sure what you want to do for the rest of your working life, you're not alone. According to a survey of worker dissatisfaction, 80 percent of working people are dissatisfied with some important area of their job or career. That's four out of five of us.

People who find themselves in unsatisfying roles are often there because they never set out to discover their most pertinent desires, nor have they catalogued their skills and abilities. The "shoulds" of life noted in Chapter 4 can cause compromise. For example, a young man decides to embrace a particular career path because somebody he respected thought he should, or because there was money to be made, or simply because an opening existed when he was looking for a job. Sometimes we change our plans and make huge life decisions with no more consideration than this.

Hopping from career to career isn't uncommon these days; it's almost becoming routine. Jobs in the United States now last an average of 4.2 years. The average person accomplishes six to eight job hunts in a lifetime and makes three career changes. One study found that 33 percent of all workers in the U.S. thought seriously about leaving their jobs within a year, and 14 percent actually left within a two-year period. Today's college graduates are armed with these statistics and go into the workplace expecting change. It's tougher for baby boomers and seniors who may hold the expectation that a job will last a lifetime. Today more than ever you need a life plan.

Frequent job turnover sometimes can be attributed to company layoffs, but many people simply become dissatisfied or even miserable, or find that they're unsuited to their work and not deriving pleasure from it. If you don't know what you want, someone may come along and sell you on a job that could potentially decimate your self-esteem and put you off track for years. With job change so prevalent, it's easy to see the value of determining your purpose. Making sure from the beginning that your work will bring satisfaction diminishes the need for change.

Careers vary as widely as the interests and abilities required. The most enjoyable kind of job for you is the work for which you're best suited. A novelist loves to write, a pianist lives for music, a statistician happily pounds out actuarial tables. Those with less-defined talents choose according to their preference from a host of business and industrial fields. Some people make unwise career choices because they're not aware of the possibilities in today's rapidly changing world. There are far more and better positions available to you than those listed in the classified ads. Some companies use headhunters, some rely on networking, and others depend on word-of-mouth for recommendations from trusted sources.

If, in the process of reading this book, you begin considering a job change, make sure that you have completed the previous chapters and thereby have investigated and identified the skills you enjoy using most. Know your areas of interest and where you want to use them. Ask yourself what kinds of environments would tap your favorite areas of knowledge. Decide exactly what kind of job you want by completing the Career Possibilities Inventory at the end of this chapter, and don't get sidetracked by thinking, "I won't find a job I'd want that I could get."

Job hunters can look through numerous lists divided into diverse career groupings. Individual lists may involve various types of skills, various work environments, and specialized vocabularies, for example. Look to libraries and schools for career resource directories such as the *Occupational Outlook Handbook* and the *Occupational Outlook Quarterly*. The *Occupational Outlook Handbook* (published every two years by the U.S. Department of Labor) contains a variety of information about occupations, educational requirements, income, and employment trends. The *Quarterly* provides a range of information, from articles depicting jobs and labor market conditions to those describing how to look for work and how to match personal aptitudes to job characteristics. Another good resource is the U.S. government's *Dictionary of Occupational Titles* (DOT), available in most local libraries, which you can use in conjunction with the *Dictionary of Holland Occupational Codes*. Ask your librarian about how to best use these sources to suit your individual purposes. Another popular tool is *What Color Is Your Parachute?* by Richard Bolles, an annually updated definitive resource for finding the right work according to your interests and abilities. Your browsing should uncover information on companies, types of professions, and sections of the country that interest you too.

As these various channels point to definite career options, proceed with decisions about education and training as you continue your research. When considering a drastic career change, the first thing most people think about is going back to school. And though this is sometimes necessary, make sure you're not relearning skills you already have.

It's important to do your homework and identify your strongest and most enjoyable skills and favorite fields of knowledge before striking out. The point is to find work that rouses passion and fully uses your aptitudes and abilities. And keep in mind that just as you must move ahead slowly in your personal growth, you shouldn't rush yourself in finding the work you love.

Shaping a career is a very personal matter. It involves goals focused on your strongest values and is successfully achieved through work that is meaningful and rewarding to you. Examine the advantages and disadvantages of every job opportunity in relation to your career aspirations. Once you have figured out what you want to do, there are many ways to approach the job market. Decide what you can offer, and plan strategies for offering advantages and services. Develop ideas of what you can successfully deliver. Concentrate on what you can give to your work and the people you want as associates.

One of the best ways to learn details about any career is to talk to people who are working in that field. Ask about every aspect of the job. If this is a new field for you, talk to at least six people you don't know, in as much depth as they will allow.

Call companies that interest you, regardless of whether there's a vacancy. Your aim is to find work that is gratifying. Rather than saying you're looking for a job, say you're interested in knowing more about the field their business represents or about their particular company. Tell them that you're information-gathering. Using this method rather than asking for a job curbs the "Sorry, no openings" response. By all means do some networking, and when you have your plan in mind, put it on paper. Make sure it gets into the hands of the right person. Companies have room for someone who can show them a definite plan of action that will benefit the company.

Career Possibilities Inventory

A. Present Work

1. How does your present job add to your life what you really need and want? _____

_____

_____

_____

_____

_____

_____

_____

_____

2. How are you able to maximize enjoyment and minimize the less pleasant activities and events?_____

_____

_____

_____

_____

_____

_____

3. Are you enjoying your work, or are you sacrificing too much? In what ways? _____

_____

_____

_____

_____

_____

4. Does your job leave time and energy for you to enjoy personal activities? If not, what's taking the time and energy?_____

_____

_____

_____

_____

_____

5. Do you want to keep your present job? Why? _____

_____

_____

_____

_____

_____

_____

B. Exploring Your Preferences

1. What type of people do you work best with? _____

_____

_____

_____

_____

_____

2. What type of work environment would you enjoy? _____

_____

_____

_____

_____

_____

3. What other working conditions would be desirable? _____

_____

_____

_____

_____

_____

4. What is your preferred level and salary? _____

_____

_____

_____

_____

5. What kind of things do you prefer to work with? _____

_____

_____

_____

_____

_____

6. What kind of information do you prefer to work with? _____

_____

_____

_____

_____

C. Ideal Career

1. What might be your job "of a lifetime"? _____

_____

_____

_____

_____

2. How would this ideal job fit into your overall life plan? _____

_____

_____

_____

_____

3. What would be necessary (previous job experience, etc.) to prepare yourself for the ideal job? _____

_____

_____

_____

_____

4. What skills would you need? Which do you already have? _____

_____

_____

_____

_____

5. Will you need to further your education? If so, what courses, degrees, or other training will you need? _____

_____

_____

_____

6. What are the possibilities for networking with people who could tell you more about the job, or who could introduce you to others who could help? _____

_____

_____

_____

Make sure that what you're planning allows you to keep your career in balance with your personal life. Don't ever get so busy making a living that you forget to make a life. A host of management studies indicate that total dedication to the job doesn't enhance your performance. And putting your career first throughout your adult life may cause you to miss out on some of your most cherished dreams. Most happy couples report that they both put each other first in the scheme of things and that their jobs come after that. Attend to your personal life. If you don't have happiness there, it will affect your work. A fulfilling personal life intensifies your ability to get more out of your career. Conversely, if you don't have a significant work identity, you'll probably have less self-esteem as a parent or marriage partner. For those with children, this "identity" doesn't necessarily mean working outside the home; rather, it's the *identification with work* that's significant: I am a writer, gardener, vocalist, chef, caretaker. These are my skills. This is what I do. Work is integral to the whole fabric of our lives and should be woven into the fabric of purpose.

Chapter 6

Sketching a Blueprint of Your Life Plan

"I would give all the wealth of the world, and all the deeds of all the heroes, for one true vision."
—Henry David Thoreau

Maybe you've backed away from creating a "life plan" in the past because you've let the term itself overwhelm you (it does sound huge and complicated, doesn't it?). Your life plan is simply an assertion of your vision and your lifelong dreams and values. It literally can be the criterion by which you measure everything else you do in your life. By making a map of the roads you want to travel in life, you'll essentially figure out where you want to go and how you expect to get there. Later on, the plan will be supported by courses of action that will bring its various elements into reality.

Through the previous chapters, you've gathered a good bit of information about yourself that's critical to writing your life plan and stating your purpose. Developing your plan is rather like stepping into the role of Sherlock Holmes. As a master detective, you'll scrutinize the clues you've uncovered and put them into a workable scenario. As psychiatrist Victor Frankl has said, we *detect* rather than *invent* our missions in life.

The bedrock of your life plan will come from the combination of your personal values, information you've uncovered about yourself, and prioritization of your needs and wants. Constructing your life plan is not unlike constructing plans for your dream house. You'd never begin by just throwing up bricks and mortar in a haphazard manner, would you? You'd carefully decide on the size of the rooms, the height of the ceilings, the look of the moldings. You'd jot ideas down on paper. You'd think and consider and visualize: the facade, the light fixtures, the colors, the building materials. You'd get a clear image of what you wanted, and then you'd develop a blueprint with construction plans before you ever turned a spadeful of dirt. In other words, you'd build the house first in your mind.

This process mirrors exactly the way to develop a life plan. Build it between your ears, and then make sure that your blueprint—your mental plan on paper—represents a clear vision of what you want. You can use your imagination to create in your mind what you hope to create in your life. It's the script before the screenplay, the conductor's vision before the concert performance, the map before the journey.

Sketching Your Blueprint

A. To begin your life-planning process, turn to the evidence and information you gleaned from the previous chapters' work. First, refer to Chapter 3, page 33, and list your five major values here:

1. _____

   _____

2. _____

   _____

3. _____

   _____

4. _____

   _____

5. _____

   _____

B. Now return to your "do-be-possess" sheets in Chapter 4 (pages 45 through 48). Prioritize each sheet by placing an "A" next to your most important entries (those you'll wish to pursue as goals). You might also want to make a "B" or "C" next to other entries. "A's" represent your highest priorities. For example, "travel to the North Star" might rank a "C," while "have a fulfilling marriage" may rank an "A." "Travel around the world" might be a "B." Do this for your entries, and make sure you indicate "A" dreams in each area (do, be, possess).

C. Once you've completed your sheets, take a few minutes to reflect on each of your "A" dreams. Using the spaces below, categorize each of these dreams under the appropriate heading:

- Personal (self-improvement, health, recreational)
- Relationship (spiritual, family, friends)
- Financial (net worth, investments, possessions)
- Career (professional accomplishments)

Personal (self-improvement, health, recreational)

_____

_____

_____

_____

_____

_____

_____

_____

_____

_____

_____

_____

_____

_____

Relationship (spiritual, family, friends)

_____

_____

_____

_____

_____

_____

_____

_____

_____

_____

_____

_____

_____

_____

_____

_____

_____

_____

Financial (net worth, investments, possessions)

_____

_____

_____

_____

_____

_____

_____

_____

_____

_____

_____

_____

_____

_____

_____

_____

_____

Career (professional accomplishments)

_____

_____

_____

_____

_____

_____

_____

_____

_____

_____

_____

_____

_____

_____

_____

_____

D. These are your most important dreams from your "do, be, possess" lists. Before going any further, look back and make sure your "A's" reflect your basic values. Once that's done, complete the Rocking Chair exercise and one or more of the other exercises before going to Chapter 7.

Exercise 1: Rocking Chair

Pretend you've reached a healthy ninety years of age. Picture yourself sitting in a rocking chair, rocking back and forth, amusing yourself by visualizing memories of days gone by. As you rock, you're thinking through your most important relationships and events. You're fascinated as the images roll by, satisfied that you've lived a good life and accomplished all that you desired. What did you do with your life? Describe it exactly as you would have wanted it:

_____

_____

_____

_____

_____

_____

_____

_____

_____

_____

_____

_____

_____

_____

_____

_____

_____

_____

_____

_____

_____

_____

_____

_____

_____

_____

_____

_____

_____

_____

_____

Now look over your response and ask yourself, "Am I spending my time on the things that will gain for me what I really want? Am I cultivating important relationships? Contributing to the greater good?" Remember, no one on their deathbed ever said, "I wish I'd put in more at the office and cleaned the house more often." What are some things you need to change or work toward if your life is to mirror the description you wrote?

Exercise 2:
Honor You

For this second exercise, picture a gathering of people who've come together to honor you. Different people from various walks of life will stand up and make comments about you and the life you've lived. The first to speak is the very closest person to you, perhaps a member of your family. What does that person say about you? Pick two others who mean a great deal to you, at least one from among your friends, and listen to their remarks. Listen carefully as they describe you. The fourth speaker is someone you've had dealings with in your business or profession. The last speaker comes from the community or your church. Take a moment and think of the comments you would cherish. What would you want accentuated about your life? What kind of friend, mother, husband, or daughter would they say you've been? What kind of professional or associate? What endearing qualities would you want remembered and what character traits emphasized?

Person 1

_____

_____

_____

_____

_____

_____

_____

_____

_____

_____

Person 2

_____
_____
_____
_____
_____
_____
_____
_____
_____
_____

Person 3

_____
_____
_____
_____
_____
_____
_____
_____
_____
_____

Person 4

_____

_____

_____

_____

_____

_____

_____

_____

_____

Person 5

_____

_____

_____

_____

_____

_____

_____

_____

_____

Look at the people who have come to honor you. If you thoughtfully considered what you wanted said, you'll see your definition of success clarified as it relates to your purpose. Is it different from what you're already striving toward? How? Be honest. Pick out some pertinent statements.

_____

_____

_____

_____

_____

_____

_____

_____

_____

_____

_____

_____

_____

_____

_____

_____

_____

Exercise 3:
Have It All

In this third exercise, imagine that you have everything you could possibly want and dream of.

Where would you be living? _____

_____

_____

_____

_____

_____

_____

_____

What work would you be doing? _____

_____

_____

_____

_____

_____

_____

_____

In what ways would you have changed? _____

_____

_____

_____

_____

_____

_____

How would you look and dress? _____

_____

_____

_____

_____

_____

Who are the people you'd have around you? _____

_____

_____

_____

_____

_____

Exercise 4:
Five Years

In this fourth exercise, answer this question:

What would be my primary goal if I only had five years to live and knew I couldn't fail?

_____

_____

_____

_____

_____

_____

_____

_____

_____

_____

_____

_____

_____

_____

_____

_____

_____

Exercise 5:
Current Identities

In this last exercise, consider the various roles you play in life—office manager, writer, parent, homemaker, investor, friend, family provider, whatever. List at least five of these roles and how you want to perform them on a day-to-day basis.

Role 1: _____

Role Statement _____

_____

Role 2: _____

Role Statement _____

_____

Role 3: _____

Role Statement _____

_____

Role 4: _____

Role Statement _____

_____

Role 5: _____

Role Statement _____

_____

Role 6: _____

Role Statement _____

_____

Role 7: _____

Role Statement _____

_____

Role 8: _____

Role Statement _____

_____

Role 9: _____

Role Statement _____

_____

Role 10: _____

Role Statement _____

_____

Congratulations—you've completed a good bit of work! And well worth it, for here you've assembled the "bricks and mortar" needed to build your life plan. You're getting a clearer mental image of the life you can construct according to your own individual specifications. Your next step is to complete the plan.

Chapter 7

Your Life Plan and Statement of Purpose

*"Great minds have purposes,
others have wishes."*
—*Washington Irving*

Your life plan and purpose aren't something you generally complete in a day's writing. You'll need time to stand apart from them, to look critically at them, to wrestle with them until you're convinced they're based on your innermost values and principles. It takes deliberation, careful analysis, and often several rewrites to produce the final draft. And once completed, you'll want to review the plan regularly, making changes as necessary to encompass new circumstances or additional insights.

In this chapter, you'll create your plan. With the completed exercises from the last chapter, you'll find ample information for constructing your life plan. Before you begin writing, review the last chapter thoroughly and:

- Concentrate on your categorized "A" dreams.

- Think through your values.

- Review your responses to the exercises.

Remember, these are important insights and the basis from which you'll create your life plan. This plan will lay the groundwork for accomplishing what you really want in life. Consider your family. Ask yourself what you want for your family and how you want to impact them. Consider your personal life, your retirement, the stepping stones to your ideal career, and anything else that's important to you. What do you want? By when do you want it?

Under "First Draft" in the exercise that follows, begin jotting down ideas of what you want for your future. Don't try for a polished product—just get some things down on paper.

Drafting Your Life Plan

A. First Draft

_____

_____

_____

_____

_____

_____

_____

_____

_____

_____

_____

_____

_____

_____

_____

_____

_____

_____

_____

A first draft should have elements that hook into your enthusiasm, that begin to get you excited. Remember, your life plan reflects what you want in life and by when you want it.

B. Second Draft

_____

_____

_____

_____

_____

_____

_____

_____

_____

_____

_____

_____

_____

_____

_____

_____

_____

_____

_____

_____

Things should be coming into focus for you now. You may want to leave this for a while. Put the task out of your conscious mind (your subconscious mind will keep working on it) and come back again later. When you review your second draft, make sure the draft reflects what you really want and when. Then begin putting together your final draft.

C. Final Draft

_____

_____

_____

_____

_____

_____

_____

_____

_____

_____

_____

_____

_____

_____

_____

_____

_____

_____

A very important part of your work is done now: You've framed your life plan. The more you acquaint yourself with it, the more it will accelerate a deeper understanding of your center and purpose, and the more it will keep you on target. Remember that your plan isn't static. It's a statement of what you want most in life—and as you change, those changes should be reflected in your plan.

Your life plan can be a dynamic all-important document for the rest of your life. What you have just created shows your direction. From here on, you won't be like the ship without a rudder that wanders aimlessly. You have your port in sight. You have the ability now to leap over years because you *know what* you want. Your deepest, most tantalizing desires stretch out before you, and now you can strategize how to get them.

Your life plan can also form the basis for a statement of purpose. Some people like to put their "raison d'être" in a nutshell. Sum it up in a sentence or two. Take their life plan and distill it into a potent essence. If that appeals to you, read on. A tightknit statement of purpose clarifies direction. Some examples follow:

- "My purpose is to create the purest foods I can, so that people can live longer, healthier lives."

- "My purpose is to affirm others, encouraging them to go for their dreams and be the best that they can be."

- "My mission is to make people laugh, so that the challenges of this earthly life don't seem quite so difficult."

- "My purpose is to create beautiful gardens, so that people may behold nature's brilliance and be happy."

- "My mission is to guide, to nurture and show love to others, most particularly those who are suffering from emotional traumas."

Writing Your Statement of Purpose

A. Before attempting to write your statement of purpose, you may want to take an uninterrupted period of quiet time to do some reflecting and jot down ideas in response to some of the following questions.

1. What do you see as your life's true purpose? _____

_____

_____

_____

_____

2. What would you need to accomplish before you died in order to live out your purpose? _____

_____

_____

_____

_____

3. What would your attitudes be? How would you have to think, speak, and act in order to bring that purpose into being? _____

_____

_____

_____

_____

_____

4. What activities would you be involved in? _____

_____

_____

_____

_____

_____

5. On a day-to-day basis, how would you live if you followed your life's
purpose completely? _____

_____

_____

_____

_____

_____

6. What habits would you have to cultivate and what would you need to
delete in order to live out your real purpose? _____

_____

_____

_____

_____

_____

B. As you write your purpose, remember to keep it simple. Draw from the questions above as well as your life plan in choosing the path before you, and name it distinctly: _____

_____

_____

_____

_____

_____

_____

Clarity of purpose and direction derive from an organized personal plan. You now have a personally developed life plan and purpose that reflect your deepest desires and dearest values. Review them periodically. Revise them as necessary.

Recommit to them frequently. Now your blueprint is completed. You can visualize the life you desire and arrange its steppingstones in harmony with the directives you've plotted out. In the next chapter, you'll begin work on transforming your life plan and purpose into reality.

Chapter 8

The Case
for Goals

"The true ideal is not opposed to the real but lies in it; and blessed are the eyes that find it."
— *James Russell Lowell*

At this point, it's obvious that you're determined not to live a mediocre life. Instead, you've chosen a life of achievement, challenge, and growth. People who've embarked upon the path you're now taking realize it isn't by chance that they know exactly what they want. They've cultivated a white-hot passion and developed a game plan. Your passion and solid plan will propel you forward too.

As you look at the life plan from which your goals will flow, be sure to think big. Big dreams birth big goals, and big goals will give you the inspiration you'll need to accomplish them. Boring goals—goals that require very little of you will leave you uninspired and cause you to quit the goal-setting process. In an experiment done with fleas, the insects were placed in a jar with a top on it. Naturally they could jump only so high or they'd hit the lid. After a while, they quit jumping as high. When the investigators finally removed the top, the fleas continued to jump only as high as the lid had allowed. Just think, with only a bit more effort, the fleas could have escaped captivity! Sound familiar? Often we humans become trained to think we can jump only so high. In reality, the possibilities are almost limitless.

You'll know you're jumping high when setting goals because risk will be involved. Big goals will always require risk. You must take some chances in life to achieve what you want. In goal setting, you're able to anticipate the risks involved and determine whether you're willing to take them. You may decide the risk is too great, and go on to pursue a different goal. Or you may find that risk adds to the excitement of overcoming obstacles to reach your desired objective.

Whichever goals you choose to pursue, make sure they demand something of you; otherwise, they won't draw out your greatest potential. So, think big, and set big goals.

Will this set you up for failure? Not at all! To build in some reassurance for yourself, you'll get immediate feedback if you mix in some smaller, more manageable goals along with the big ones. Meanwhile, the exciting big goals will keep you inspired and percolating. What a self-esteem booster when you accomplish some small goals that are leading to the big ones!

Creating Dream-Inspired Goals

To create your dream-inspired goals, here's the process you should follow:

1. Review your categorized "A" dream sheets on pages 64 through 67. In each category (Personal, Relationship, etc.), note whether each dream is long range (extending beyond two years), mid-range (a month to two years), or short range (a day to a few weeks).

2. Next transfer the "A" dreams you categorized in #1 above to the appropriate Long-Range, Mid-Range, and Short-Range dream sheets on pages 92-94.

3. Add to the lists by reviewing your life plan on page 83 and your purpose statement on page 87. Make sure that all of your "blueprint" is included.

4. Once completed, you can create goals from these lists.

A. Long-Range Dreams (beyond two years)

_____
_____
_____
_____
_____
_____
_____
_____
_____
_____
_____
_____
_____
_____
_____
_____
_____
_____
_____
_____
_____

B. Mid-Range Dreams (a month to two years)

_____

_____

_____

_____

_____

_____

_____

_____

_____

_____

_____

_____

_____

_____

_____

_____

_____

_____

_____

_____

_____

_____

C. Short-Range Dreams (a day to a few weeks)

_____

_____

_____

_____

_____

_____

_____

_____

_____

_____

_____

_____

_____

_____

_____

_____

_____

_____

_____

_____

A goal is an end that one strives to attain. An end. A desired result. Not *how* you're going to do something, or a vague description of what it will feel like, but a definite, quantifiable outcome. Something an objective observer could attest to. Practice phrasing your goals in action statements, as something you intend to accomplish. Just as importantly, goals must have target dates for accomplishment. This is an integral part of goal setting. Be realistic, yet set a time frame that will get you moving immediately. If you fall behind, you can always adjust the date. Remember: *You* are the master of your goals, not the other way around! To make your goals definite and quantifiable, write them as specifically as possible. For example, compare the "vague" and "specific" versions of the following goals:

Vague	Specific
People will like me more.	I will cultivate three friendships over the next six months.
I'll look better.	I will lose fifteen pounds by December 31.
I will make more money.	I will earn $100,000 this year.

One way to check yourself is to ask, "How will I know when I get there?" for each statement you write; the answer should be obvious ("when I lose fifteen pounds").

Writing Goal Statements

To begin generating goals for yourself, take the following steps:

1. Review your list of long-, mid-, and short-range dreams.

2. Pick six dreams, possibly two from each list (long, mid, short). For balance, make sure the dreams pertain to most of the areas of your life (personal, relationship, financial, and career).

3. Write out a specific goal statement for each dream. Make it a quantifiable action statement with a target date. For example, if your dream is: "I want to be a published author," your goal may be worded something like this: "I will complete a first draft of my book by March 3."

Dream: _____

_____

Goal statement no. 1: _____

_____

_____

_____

Dream: _____

_____

Goal statement no. 2: _____

_____

_____

_____

Dream: _____

_____

Goal statement no. 3: _____

_____

_____

_____

Dream: _____

_____

Goal statement no. 4: _____

_____

_____

_____

Dream: _____

_____

Goal statement no. 5: _____

_____

_____

_____

Dream: _____

_____

Goal statement no. 6: _____

_____

_____

_____

Now that your goals are crystallizing and you know what you're aiming for in life, you can complete "Goal Sheets" for each of your six goal statements (see pages 100-111). Select one of your goals and write a goal statement at the top of the sheet. Drop down to "Challenges I Face" and think about possible obstacles you'll have to overcome. List them on the sheet in the space provided.

Now, under "Prioritized Action Steps," create an action list. That is, write what you need to do in order to bring this goal about as well as a target date for each action. Here's an example:

Goal:

I will locate an agent to represent my screenplay.

Action List:

I will obtain an agent listing with addresses.	Sept. 1
I will create a phone script.	Sept. 3
I will create a cover letter for the screenplay.	Sept. 10
I will contact twenty agents.	Oct. 1
I will mail out fifteen screenplays.	Oct. 10
I will follow up with all agents contacted.	Nov. 10

Action steps clarify and simplify goals, particularly large or long-term ones, by giving you something manageable to aim at. As you take each definite step, you will experience a sense of accomplishment and be propelled to complete your goal. You'll be like the ant that devours the elephant, or the wave that carves out a cove. Persistence and determination are necessary qualities for accomplishing goals. Take one of your large goals, possibly a long-term one, and break it into more attainable bite-sized pieces. Write them down as action steps.

Once you have put each goal into a measurable statement, complete with target date, obstacles to overcome, actions to accomplish, and benefits to you and others, make the decision to commit to this goal. Don't take it lightly. Use this checklist to test your commitment:

- Am I truly willing to do what's necessary to reach this goal?

- Is the goal worthy of the time I'll invest?

- Are the spoils worth the cost of the hunt?

- Does the goal fit snugly into my life plan?

If you answered "yes" to each question, sign your name at the bottom of the Goal Sheet to indicate you are committed to this goal. You're making a contract—and it's of utmost importance to be true to yourself. Finally, document your progress by recording the actions you have accomplished. This keeps you on track and excited as you see yourself approaching your goal.

Goal Sheet #1

Today's date _____   Final target date _____

                                                   Date achieved _____

A. Goal statement (written positively and specifically): _____

_____

_____

_____

B. Challenges I face (obstacles to overcome): _____

_____

_____

_____

C. Prioritized action steps (what I plan to do and when I plan to do it):

                            Step   *Completed by*

_____   _____

_____   _____

_____   _____

_____   _____

_____   _____

_____   _____

_____   _____

D. Benefits of achieving this goal (for me and for others; affirmation statements):

To me _____

_____

_____

_____

_____

_____

_____

To others _____

_____

_____

_____

_____

_____

E. Commitment: Is this goal worth the time, effort, and money it will take me to reach it?   ☐ Yes   ☐ No

Signature: _____

Goal Sheet #2

Today's date _____   Final target date _____

Date achieved _____

A. Goal statement (written positively and specifically): _____

_____

_____

_____

B. Challenges I face (obstacles to overcome): _____

_____

_____

_____

C. Prioritized action steps (what I plan to do and when I plan to do it):

Step	*Completed by*
_____	_____
_____	_____
_____	_____
_____	_____
_____	_____
_____	_____
_____	_____

D. Benefits of achieving this goal (for me and for others; affirmation statements):

To me _____

_____

_____

_____

_____

_____

To others _____

_____

_____

_____

_____

_____

E. Commitment: Is this goal worth the time, effort, and money it will take me to reach it? ☐ Yes ☐ No

Signature: _____

Goal Sheet #3

Today's date _____   Final target date _____

Date achieved _____

A. Goal statement (written positively and specifically): _____

_____

_____

_____

B. Challenges I face (obstacles to overcome): _____

_____

_____

_____

C. Prioritized action steps (what I plan to do and when I plan to do it):

Step   *Completed by*

_____   _____

_____   _____

_____   _____

_____   _____

_____   _____

_____   _____

_____   _____

D. Benefits of achieving this goal (for me and for others; affirmation statements):

To me _____

_____

_____

_____

_____

_____

_____

To others _____

_____

_____

_____

_____

_____

_____

E. Commitment: Is this goal worth the time, effort, and money it will take me to reach it? ☐ Yes ☐ No

Signature: _____

Goal Sheet #4

Today's date _____   Final target date _____

Date achieved _____

A. Goal statement (written positively and specifically): _____

_____

_____

_____

B. Challenges I face (obstacles to overcome): _____

_____

_____

_____

C. Prioritized action steps (what I plan to do and when I plan to do it):

Step	Completed by
_____	_____
_____	_____
_____	_____
_____	_____
_____	_____
_____	_____
_____	_____

D. Benefits of achieving this goal (for me and for others; affirmation statements):

To me _____

_____

_____

_____

_____

_____

_____

To others _____

_____

_____

_____

_____

_____

_____

E. Commitment: Is this goal worth the time, effort, and money it will take me to reach it? ☐ Yes   ☐ No

Signature: _____

Goal Sheet #5

Today's date _____   Final target date _____

Date achieved _____

A. Goal statement (written positively and specifically): _____

_____

_____

_____

B. Challenges I face (obstacles to overcome): _____

_____

_____

_____

C. Prioritized action steps (what I plan to do and when I plan to do it):

Step	*Completed by*
_____	_____
_____	_____
_____	_____
_____	_____
_____	_____
_____	_____
_____	_____

D. Benefits of achieving this goal (for me and for others; affirmation statements):

To me _____

_____

_____

_____

_____

_____

To others _____

_____

_____

_____

_____

_____

E. Commitment: Is this goal worth the time, effort, and money it will take me to reach it?　☐ Yes　☐ No

Signature: _____

Goal Sheet #6

Today's date _____   Final target date _____

Date achieved _____

A. Goal statement (written positively and specifically): _____

_____

_____

_____

B. Challenges I face (obstacles to overcome): _____

_____

_____

_____

C. Prioritized action steps (what I plan to do and when I plan to do it):

Step	*Completed by*
_____	_____
_____	_____
_____	_____
_____	_____
_____	_____
_____	_____
_____	_____

D. Benefits of achieving this goal (for me and for others; affirmation statements):

To me _____

_____

_____

_____

_____

_____

_____

To others _____

_____

_____

_____

_____

_____

_____

E. Commitment: Is this goal worth the time, effort, and money it will take me to reach it? ☐ Yes ☐ No

Signature: _____

There are many strategies for reaching your goals. Visualization, for example, is a powerful tool that you will explore in the next chapter. A very simple strategy that is also quite effective is to write each of your goals on a 3" x 5" card, which makes for handy review. On the back, you can write all the reasons you must achieve this goal, and what will happen if you don't. This is the carrot-and-stick approach: By writing why you must achieve this goal, you are adding fuel to your desire, and your desire will propel you to the accomplishment of your dreams.

By writing what will happen if you don't achieve this goal, you are utilizing another powerful force for your own good: disappointment. You are creating in your mind a great need for this goal as well as what you stand to lose should you not achieve it. This is an excellent way to influence your behavior.

Finally, it is helpful to gather support material for your goals. Pictures of that Italian villa you wish to own. Articles on the happy family life you want to create. These "success clues" will keep your mind working on how to reach those goals.

By reviewing your goals monthly, weekly, or daily, you'll be working with your subconscious mind to bring them into reality. Your brain will work toward reaching the goal as long as it knows what target to shoot for!

Chapter 9

Visualization and Thought-Talk

*"Believe that life is worth living, and
your belief will help create the fact."*
—William James

The power of your belief system is immense—it influences choices, decisions, goals, even your life's direction. You unconsciously make belief-assumptions about yourself all the time: "This is who I am. Here's what I can do. This is what people think of me. This is what I should earn. This doesn't work. That's out of my reach." Your self-image—your mental opinion of yourself—rises and falls on what you think of yourself. Your success, therefore, begins with your beliefs.

Negative beliefs about yourself engender negative self-talk, and together the two persuade you that you're incapable of things that in fact you may be quite capable of doing. They may actually block your ability to perform. People who have convinced themselves that nothing good is going to happen, or that they can't do anything with their lives because of their past are right! Whether you believe you can or believe you can't, you're generally right on target. And a great deal has to do with what you tell yourself. If you tell yourself you can't, if you feed yourself images of helplessness—"I'll never be successful" or "I can't do it"—you'll be immobilized, paralyzed, unable to move forward. Even if you have the skills and necessary resources, once you tell yourself you can't, you restrict your ability to proceed.

On the other hand, positive thought-talk has the opposite effect. If you tell yourself you can do something, the whole idea becomes more plausible, and you open avenues that pave the way to achievement. It's generally accepted that people reap what they sow. Say you decide to make a garden. You prepare the soil and plant seeds of your favorite spring flowers. Next comes fertilizer, plus adequate sun and water. What do you expect to burst forth from the ground? Your favorite spring flowers, of course! If you had planted poison ivy or deadly nightshade, now what would you expect to grow? Spring flowers? Of course not! You reap what you sow.

If we plant negative thoughts and then water them with images of inadequacy and impotency, then we're most certainly sowing failure—and we will reap it in the end. In many ways, our thoughts and images of ourselves and our circumstances act as self-fulfilling prophecies. If you have an image of yourself as bright and articulate, for example, you'll tend to speak well and easily. If you have the opposite view, you'll tend to portray and describe yourself to others negatively. Thus the self-fulfilling prophecy becomes a reality.

You have control of but one thing, and that is your thoughts. It takes self-discipline and habit to control them. Keeping your mind busy with a definite purpose underlined by a definite plan is the most practical way to form the habit. People who achieve notable success have this kind of control; they apply their thoughts to attaining their objectives.

It's difficult to change your behavior unless you change the inner picture. Here you must be diligent and watchful: watchful by staying aware of what's going on in your mind and diligent to deal with negative thoughts by scuttling them and consciously turning your mind to something else. It's possible to change your attitude by refocusing your mind.

In contemplating change, consider ditching all the "shoulds" and "oughts" and using good strong "want-to's." Instead of "I should lose this ugly fat," give your diet plan a "want-to" such as "I want to be slender because…" then list reasons: "I'm going to look better, feel better, and my friends will notice. I'll get compliments. The money I'd spend for that cake can go right into my fund for a new pair of jeans to show off my slim, new self."

Want-to's are energizing. Ought-to's drag us down. If you want to have a rewarding career, look a particular way, develop a certain lifestyle, or accomplish the goals you've identified, you'll need a large-sized "want-to." You'll like using "want-to's" when you see yourself attracting, looking like, and having what you want.

The best way to forecast your future is to create it by using the time-tested tools discussed so far and bathing your goals in positive belief and affirmative imaging. One of the most often-quoted statements about visualization comes from Dr. Maxwell Maltz in his well-known *Psycho-Cybernetics:* "Our subconscious mind can't tell the difference between a real experience and one that has been vividly imagined." The subconscious mind acts as a servant to its conscious counterpart. The subconscious works in this capacity to bring into being what the conscious mind has shown it. "What you see is what you get." Whether it's real or imagined doesn't matter; the conscious mind thinks it, visualizes it, and marks it with a value judgment, and the subconscious mind attempts to bring it about.

There's nothing magical or mystical about this. People in all walks of life use creative imaging to accomplish their goals. Olympic athletes visualize themselves winning the race, scoring the touchdown, or performing with skill and accuracy—before the competition begins. Professional speakers envision their audiences responding to a superb performance. Sales managers encourage staff members to imagine themselves making the sale before they meet with clients. Patients who visualize and think positively about their healing are more likely to mend rapidly and with less hardship. You likely used this same power of artistic imaging to plan your own reality—both quality and scope—before you set your goals. What you visualize and say to yourself does make a difference. If you focus on high-value outcomes, you're more likely to have them. It's easier to achieve something you can visualize and describe in a manner that's personally believable. The pictures and thoughts you see in your mind will have a powerful effect on your personal achievement.

So, develop inner images of the outcomes you expect to reach. Consciously decide what you want. When your mind has a clearly conceived, credible focal point, it can aim and evaluate, then aim again and reevaluate, until it reaches the intended target. Focus like this gives your mind a clear picture to disseminate information that will lead you closer to your goal.

There are many ways to envision a goal. Picture it in your mind, or enhance the image by drawing it out and sketching yourself into it. Use the 3" x 5" card method, or write out a statement of accomplishment that you can paste to your bathroom mirror or steering wheel or carry in your pocket—wherever you'll read it frequently. Memorize and repeat the statement throughout the day. You can also affect change by identifying yourself with a particular image that will inspire you to continue seeking your aim. This could be a slogan, a symbol, or the physical and mental pictures that are meaningful to you. Become interactive with your goal. If your objective is a new home, drive through nice neighborhoods to get ideas. Ask yourself, "How did these people acquire these lovely homes and beautiful surroundings?" Most of them planned and worked to make their dreams come true. The point is, give yourself a target, and program your mind every day through explicit, visual messages that this is your actuality.

To attain your goals, you must be able to see yourself functioning comfortably in them. Visualization and belief allow you to do this—to become comfortable in the imagined reality before it becomes your here and now. And it's these two components—visualization and belief—that keep you focusing on high-quality outcomes. The more you can tune into these outcomes, the more inspired you'll be to take steps toward fulfilling your goals and attaining your purpose.

Chapter 10

Reflecting on the Process

"How pleasant it is, at the end of the day, No follies to have to repent; But reflect on the past, and be able to say, That my time has been happily spent."
　　—Jane Taylor
　　Rhymes for the Nursery,
　　The Way to Be Happy

You get more out of your "purpose" if you truly use your talents and abilities, if you manage your time well to accomplish your goals, and if you live for something greater than yourself. Abraham Maslow, a primary framer of modern psychology, has identified self-actualization as the highest step in human experience. According to Dr. Maslow, you arrive at that pinnacle by moving along and satisfying each step of a hierarchy of needs. Once operating in the self-actualizing mode, you're set free to find your niche, to do what you love, to make deliberate choices, and to cultivate work that would be most personally fulfilling. Later Maslow acknowledged a plateau higher than self-actualization—a step he called "self-transcendence"—that is necessary to find true satisfaction in life. He described self-transcendence as living for a purpose *greater than oneself.* Meaning comes from contribution, from living for something higher. There is a need for having a higher purpose.

We all need something that moves us, that stirs our passions. We need to make a dent by doing something we're good at and enjoy. We need to feel useful in serving others in a cause. We're designed to find satisfaction through contributing to the greater good. Probably the greatest fulfillment in improving ourselves comes through being able to more skillfully reach out and touch others, to do what we can by being kinder, more grateful, and more peaceful, productive, and loving. In other words, to make this earth a better place to live.

The pursuit of your purpose will be far more satisfying if you're using your talents and your abilities. We hope to discover that we are set apart by some inherent distinction, something that causes us to satisfy a calling no one else can meet. We hope for answers to our question: "Is there a destiny for me to fulfill?" Many trust that their answers will ultimately come from the world around them, in good time. There are countless other people who attest to their spiritual faith as a powerful source of direction and purpose. Regardless of your personal predisposition, you'll always be most fulfilled when your purpose is one that best suits the world and best suits you as well. To be able to say, "Life has deep meaning to me now—I've discovered my own true mission" leaves you energized and fulfilled, and your efforts that much more worthwhile.

It's extremely easy to get caught up in a tangle of activities, allowing the "urgent" to run our lives. When this happens, every step takes us rapidly in the wrong direction. Successes are empty and come at the expense of what really matters most. How very different life is when you've determined your purpose and its value, and you visualize and keep it before you daily. You know where you're going when you have a clear understanding of your destination, and when you focus your energies on what's deeply important. You organize yourself to do and be what matters most according to your purpose and you order your steps accordingly. Each segment of your life, then—what you do today, what you do tomorrow, next week, next month— can be reviewed in advance, relative to your overall plan. If you keep that end in mind on a daily basis, you can make sure that none of your values are violated, that you are aligned with your purpose, and that each day of your life contributes in a significant way to the vision you have of your life as a whole.

Bibliography and Suggested Reading

Bender, David. *Constructing a Life Philosophy: Opposing Viewpoints*. St. Paul, MN: Greenhaven Press, 1985.

Bennett, Robert F., Kurt Hanks, and Gerreld L. Pulsipher. *Gaining Control*. Salt Lake City, UT: Franklin Institute, 1987.

Bolles, Richard Nelson. *What Color Is Your Parachute?* Berkeley, CA: Ten Speed Press, 1994.

Braham, Barbara J. *Finding Your Purpose: A Guide to Personal Fulfillment*. Los Altos, CA: Crisp Publications, 1991.

Bristol, Claude M., and Harold Sherman. *TNT, The Power Within You: How to Release the Forces Inside You—And Get What You Want!* Englewood Cliffs, NJ: Prentice Hall, 1982.

Carr-Ruffino, Norma. *The Promotable Woman: Advancing Through Leadership Skills*. Belmont, CA: Wadsworth, 1985.

Chapman, Elmwood L. *Attitude: Your Most Priceless Possession*. Los Altos, CA: Crisp Publications, 1990.

Covey, Stephen, A. Roger Merrill, and Rebecca R. Merrill. *First Things First: To Live, to Love, to Learn, to Leave a Legacy*. New York: Simon & Schuster, 1994.

Covey, Stephen. *The Seven Habits of Highly Effective People: Restoring the Character Ethic*. New York: Simon & Schuster, 1989.

Crystal, John C., and Richard N. Bolles. *Where Do I Go From Here With My Life? A Very Systematic, Practical, and Effective Life/Work Planning Manual for Students, Instructors, Counselors, Career Seekers and Career Changes*. Berkeley, CA: Ten Speed Press, 1974.

Dahl, Dan, and Randolph Sikes. *Charting Your Goals: Personal Life-Goals Planner: Self-Directed Exercises That Will Help You Achieve Your Personal and Business Objectives in the Areas of Career, Health, Relationships, Finances, Personal Growth, and Values Clarification*. New York: Perennial Library, 1988.

Gottfredson, Gary D., and John L. Holland. *Dictionary of Holland Occupational Codes*. Lutz, FL: Psychological Acess Resources, Inc., 1989.

Hill, Napoleon, and W. Clement Stone. *Success Through a Positive Mental Attitude*. New York: Prentice Hall, 1977.

Hill, Napoleon. *Think and Grow Rich*. New York: Fawcett Crest, 1960.

Katz, Dr. Stan J., and Aimee E. Liu. *Success Trap: Rethink Your Ambitions to Achieve Greater Personal and Professional Fulfillment*. New York: Ticknor & Fields, 1990.

Lennox, Joan Hatch, and Judith Hatch Shapiro. *Life Changes: How Women Can Make Courageous Choices*. New York: Crown, 1990.

Maltz, Maxwell. *Psycho-Cybernetics*. New York: Pocket Books, 1969.

Maslow, Abraham. *Toward A Psychology of Being*. New York: Van Nostrand Reinhold, 1968.

Robbins, Anthony. *Awaken the Giant Within: How to Take Immediate Control of Your Mental, Emotional, Physical and Financial Destiny*. New York: Summit Books, 1991.

Robbins, Anthony. *Unlimited Power*. New York: Fawcett Columbine, 1987.

Rubin, Theodore Isaac. *Overcoming Indecisiveness: The Eight Stages of Effective Decision Making*. New York: Harper & Row, 1984.

Schwartz, David. *The Magic of Getting What You Want*. New York: W. Morrow, 1987.

Sher, Barbara. *Wishcraft: How to Get What You Really Want*. New York: Viking Press, 1979.

Sinetar, Marsha. *Do What You Love, The Money Will Follow: Discovering Your Right Livelihood*. New York: Dell Publishing, 1989.

Stoddard, Alexandra. *Living A Beautiful Life: Five Hundred Ways to Add Elegance, Order, Beauty, and Joy to Every Day of Your Life*. New York: Random House, 1986.

Thoreau, Henry David. *On Walden Pond*. New York: Bramhall House, 1951.

Timm, Paul R. *Successful Self-Management: A Psychologically Sound Approach to Personal Effectiveness*. Los Altos, CA: Crisp Publications, 1990.

U.S. Department of Labor. *Occupational Outlook Handbook*. Washington, D.C.: Bureau of Labor Statistics, U.S. Government Printing Office, 1994.

U.S. Department of Labor. *Occupational Outlook Quarterly*. Washington, D.C.: Bureau of Labor Statistics, U.S. Government Printing Office, 1995.

U.S. Department of Labor. *Dictionary of Occupational Titles.* 4th ed. Lanham, MD: Employment and Training Administration, Bernan Press, 1991.

Willingham, Ron. *When Good Isn't Good Enough.* New York: Doubleday, 1989.

Ziglar, Zig. *See You at the Top.* Gretna, LA: Pelican Publishing, 1989.

Available From SkillPath Publications

Self-Study Sourcebooks

Climbing the Corporate Ladder: What You Need to Know and Do to Be a Promotable Person *by Barbara Pachter and Marjorie Brody*

Coping With Supervisory Nightmares: 12 Common Nightmares of Leadership and What You Can Do About Them *by Michael and Deborah Singer Dobson*

Defeating Procrastination: 52 Fail-Safe Tips for Keeping Time on Your Side *by Marlene Caroselli, Ed.D.*

Discovering Your Purpose *by Ivy Haley*

Going for the Gold: Winning the Gold Medal for Financial Independence *by Lesley D. Bissett, CFP*

Having Something to Say When You Have to Say Something: The Art of Organizing Your Presentation *by Randy Horn*

Info-Flood: How to Swim in a Sea of Information Without Going Under *by Marlene Caroselli, Ed.D.*

The Innovative Secretary *by Marlene Caroselli, Ed.D.*

Letters & Memos: Just Like That! *by Dave Davies*

Mastering the Art of Communication: Your Keys to Developing a More Effective Personal Style *by Michelle Fairfield Poley*

Organized for Success! 95 Tips for Taking Control of Your Time, Your Space, and Your Life *by Nanci McGraw*

A Passion to Lead! How to Develop Your Natural Leadership Ability *by Michael Plumstead*

P.E.R.S.U.A.D.E.: Communication Strategies That Move People to Action *by Marlene Caroselli, Ed.D.*

Productivity Power: 250 Great Ideas for Being More Productive *by Jim Temme*

Promoting Yourself: 50 Ways to Increase Your Prestige, Power, and Paycheck *by Marlene Caroselli, Ed.D.*

Proof Positive: How to Find Errors Before They Embarrass You *by Karen L. Anderson*

Risk-Taking: 50 Ways to Turn Risks Into Rewards *by Marlene Caroselli, Ed.D. and David Harris*

Speak Up and Stand Out: How to Make Effective Presentations *by Nanci McGraw*

Stress Control: How You Can Find Relief From Life's Daily Stress *by Steve Bell*

The Technical Writer's Guide *by Robert McGraw*

Total Quality Customer Service: How to Make It Your Way of Life *by Jim Temme*

Write It Right! A Guide for Clear and Correct Writing *by Richard Andersen and Helene Hinis*

Your Total Communication Image *by Janet Signe Olson, Ph.D.*

Handbooks

The ABC's of Empowered Teams: Building Blocks for Success *by Mark Towers*

Assert Yourself! Developing Power-Packed Communication Skills to Make Your Points Clearly, Confidently, and Persuasively *by Lisa Contini*

Breaking the Ice: How to Improve Your On-the-Spot Communication Skills *by Deborah Shouse*

The Care and Keeping of Customers: A Treasury of Facts, Tips, and Proven Techniques for Keeping Your Customers Coming BACK! *by Roy Lantz*

Challenging Change: Five Steps for Dealing With Change *by Holly DeForest and Mary Steinberg*

Dynamic Delegation: A Manager's Guide for Active Empowerment *by Mark Towers*

Every Woman's Guide to Career Success *by Denise M. Dudley*

Grammar? No Problem! *by Dave Davies*

Great Openings and Closings: 28 Ways to Launch and Land Your Presentations With Punch, Power, and Pizazz *by Mari Pat Varga*

Hiring and Firing: What Every Manager Needs to Know *by Marlene Caroselli, Ed.D. with Laura Wyeth, Ms.Ed.*

How to Be a More Effective Group Communicator: Finding Your Role and Boosting Your Confidence in Group Situations *by Deborah Shouse*

How to Deal With Difficult People *by Paul Friedman*

Learning to Laugh at Work: The Power of Humor in the Workplace *by Robert McGraw*

Making Your Mark: How to Develop a Personal Marketing Plan for Becoming More Visible and More Appreciated at Work *by Deborah Shouse*

Meetings That Work *by Marlene Caroselli, Ed.D.*

The Mentoring Advantage: How to Help Your Career Soar to New Heights *by Pam Grout*

Minding Your Business Manners: Etiquette Tips for Presenting Yourself Professionally in Every Business Situation *by Marjorie Brody and Barbara Pachter*

Misspeller's Guide *by Joel and Ruth Schroeder*

Motivation in the Workplace: How to Motivate Workers to Peak Performance and Productivity *by Barbara Fielder*

NameTags Plus: Games You Can Play When People Don't Know What to Say *by Deborah Shouse*

Networking: How to Creatively Tap Your People Resources *by Colleen Clarke*

New & Improved! 25 Ways to Be More Creative and More Effective *by Pam Grout*

Power Write! A Practical Guide to Words That Work *by Helene Hinis*

The Power of Positivity: Eighty ways to energize your life *by Joel and Ruth Schroeder*

Putting Anger to Work For You *by Ruth and Joel Schroeder*

Reinventing Your Self: 28 Strategies for Coping With Change *by Mark Towers*

Saying "No" to Negativity: How to Manage Negativity in Yourself, Your Boss, and Your Co-Workers *by Zoie Kaye*

The Supervisor's Guide: The Everyday Guide to Coordinating People and Tasks *by Jerry Brown and Denise Dudley, Ph.D.*

Taking Charge: A Personal Guide to Managing Projects and Priorities *by Michal E. Feder*

Treasure Hunt: 10 Stepping Stones to a New and More Confident You! *by Pam Grout*

A Winning Attitude: How to Develop Your Most Important Asset! *by Michelle Fairfield Poley*

For more information, call 1-800-873-7545.

Notes

Notes

Notes

Notes

Notes

Notes